ISBN 978-1-334-48133-8
PIBN 10726941

1 MONTH OF FREE READING

at

www.ForgottenBooks.com

By purchasing this book you are eligible for one month membership to ForgottenBooks.com, giving you unlimited access to our entire collection of over 700,000 titles via our web site and mobile apps.

To claim your free month visit:

www.forgottenbooks.com/free726941

English
Français
Deutsche
Italiano
Español
Português

www.forgottenbooks.com

Mythology Photography **Fiction**
Fishing Christianity **Art** Cooking
Essays Buddhism Freemasonry
Medicine **Biology** Music **Ancient**
Egypt Evolution Carpentry Physics
Dance Geology **Mathematics** Fitness
Shakespeare **Folklore** Yoga Marketing
Confidence Immortality Biographies
Poetry **Psychology** Witchcraft
Electronics Chemistry History **Law**
Accounting **Philosophy** Anthropology
Alchemy Drama Quantum Mechanics
Atheism Sexual Health **Ancient History**
Entrepreneurship Languages Sport
Paleontology Needlework Islam
Metaphysics Investment Archaeology
Parenting Statistics Criminology
Motivational

THE

WONDERFUL WATER CURE.

AN OPERATIC EXTRAVAGANZA,

𝔈n 𝔒ne 𝔄ct,

BY

B. WEBSTER, Comedian,

(MEMBER OF THE DRAMATIC AUTHORS' SOCIETY,)

AS PERFORMED AT THE

THEATRE ROYAL, HAY-MARKET.

CORRECTLY PRINTED FROM THE PROMPTER'S COPY, WITH
THE CAST OF CHARACTERS, COSTUME, SCENIC
ARRANGEMENT, SIDES OF ENTRANCE AND EXIT,
AND RELATIVE POSITIONS OF THE
DRAMATIS PERSONÆ.

SPLENDIDLY ILLUSTRATED WITH AN ENGRAVING
BY MR. BREWER,
TAKEN DURING THE REPRESENTATION OF THE PIECE.

LONDON:

PUBLISHED AT THE NATIONAL ACTING DRAMA OFFICE, 19
SUFFOLK STREET, PALL MALL, EAST; "NASSAU STEAM PRESS,"
60, ST. MARTIN'S LANE, CHARING CROSS; TO BE HAD OF
STRANGE, PATERNOSTER ROW; WISEHEART, SUFFOLK STREET,
DUBLIN; AND ALL RESPECTABLE BOOKSELLERS.

Dramatis Personæ and Costume.

First Performed Wednesday, July 15th, 1846.

TARTAGLIA—1st Dress: Crimson velvet coat, handsomely trimmed, green velvet trousers, handsomely trimmed, amber satin waistcoat, handsomely trimmed, high black boots, scarlet tops, cock hat and feather trimming. 2nd Dress; Morning gown and cap . . . . } MR. PAUL BEDFORD.

BELLONI—1st Dress: Black coat, handsomely trimmed, satin waistcoat, handsomely trimmed, pink silk breeches, cock hat. 2nd Dress: black dress trimmed white, pierrot . . } MR. HUDSON.

THE PODESTA—Black suit, and grand cock hat . . . . . } MR. JAMES BLAND.

ADONIS—Old fashioned livery. . MR. ELLIS.

POLICHINELLE—Dress . . . MR. ENNIS.

ARGENTINE—White satin upper dress, red satin brocaded petticoat, silver tissue hat . . . . . } MADAME ANNA THILLON.

Chorus as Italian Peasants.

Peasantry, jacket and coats old fashioned.

Time of representation, fifty minutes.

EXPLANATION OF THE STAGE DIRECTIONS.

L. means first entrance, left. R. first entrance, right. S.E.L. second entrance, left. S.E.R. second entrance, right. U.E.L. upper entrance, left. U.E.R. upper entrance, right. C. centre. L.C. left centre. R.C. right centre. T.E.L. third entrance, left. T.E.R. third entrance, right. Observing you are supposed to face the audience.

THE WONDERFUL WATER CURE.

SCENE.—*A public place in Naples—a fountain in* C. *at back—a platform, with steps ascending to it, and booth,* R. *with a sign, on which is written "*TARTAGLIA, *physician in ordinary to the great Cham of Tartary."—In the centre of the booth, a opening in the canvas leading on to the raised stage, a opening on the return side of the booth facing the audience below. A similar booth,* L., *with a sign, on which is written "*SCARAMOUCH, *dentist to the Queen of Congo," round a Negro's head, and two elephant's tusks—a trumpet on the balustrade,* R.—*a gong on balustrade,* L.—*break of day, during the duet the sun gradually rises.*

Enter BELLONI, U. E. L., *with an umbrella,.*

DUET.

When all around reposing,
    Here lover-like I stray,
While morn's red lip unclosing,
    Awakes the smiling day.
The echo of the mountain
    No plaint from *me* ere hears—
Nor do I fill the fountain
    With torrents of my tears;
For I'm no child of sorrow—
    A strolling play'r by trade;
So all my tears I borrow—
    My groans are ready made.
Inconstancy has never
    Undone my peace of rest,
For hope and gladness ever
    Have dealt within my heart.

Enter ARGENTINE, *from opening of booth below* R.

Arg.

How gayly once and lightly
    I trolled the fields along,
When rose the lark, so sprightly,
    Invoked his matin song;

But now at night, no sleeping—
  My heart keeps me awake—
My morning's passed in weeping,
  As tho' my heart would break,
And yet, I know he loves me,
  He bids me not despair—
Tho' cruel fate would parts us,
  Is he not ever there?
Is hope denied then ever?
  Can I then never rest?
Must drooping sorrow never
  Relieve my aching heart?

Bel.   Come, gentle love,
    Angel above,
Dwell in her heart,
  Come, gentle love.

Arg.   Go, cruel love,
    Elsewhere to rove—
Leave me to rest,
  Go, cruel love.
Ah, it is he—great pow'r.

Bel. Argentine, my dearest—
Arg. Belloni, at this hour?
Bel. Loveliest and dearest.
Arg: Wherefore return you here?
Bel. Oh, ask me sooner, love,
  Why seeks the sun, the flower,
    And lifts its head above?
  It seeks like me, one hour
    Of love—brief life of love.

Arg. Yes, yes, I do believe thee,
    Joy flutters thro' my breast—
No, no, you'd ne'er deceive me,
    Yes, dearest, yes, and best!

Bel. Dearest Argentine,
My love's only queen!
My heart's only thine!
None shall ever thwart us!
None shall ever part us!
You shall be only mine!

Arg. Thine own Argentine
Ever true has been,
Her heart's ever thine!
Cruel fate will thwart us—
Shall they ever part us?
Thou art ever mine.

Bel. Yes, thou'rt mine!
Yes, mine—for ever mine!

> My only, only love !
> Thou'rt mine ! thou'rt mine !

Bel.   Dear Argentine,
> Can fairer be seen
> Than she, that is mine !
> Dear Argentine !

Arg.   In dreams of thee,
> Dear Belloni,
> I am thine ! I am thine ·
> Dreaming of thee !

Bel. Last night I informed that old Charlatan, your guardian, of my honourable views towards you. I, the great scaramouch of Naples—the renowned Belloni, before whose stage princes stop and shake—with laughter. I offered to endow you, with my name and myself—would you believe it? he refused; but do not be alarmed, you shall be mine, in spite of his determination to wed you himself, by fair means or foul !

Arg. Would he dare ?

Bel. Compose yourself—I will pay him off. But tell me, how do you manage to draw on existence when I'm away ?

Arg. Well, must I confess the truth—ah-heigho !—it's a sad fact; but gaily enough !

Bel. Gaily ! ah, traitress !

Arg. Oh ! but do not forget, if I dance, laugh, sing and play; it is, alas, my wretched trade to feign a joy, I am far from feeling—like the decoy bird the fowler's use, my song is but a deceit.

AIR.

At break of day, a lone nightingale,
     Have you never heard, when some place her song
To bait a net, with notes which never fail,
     Warbling, to draw from the grove, all the tuneful throng.
Captive she—captive tho' she be,
One brief hour thinks she is free.
Her sweet note, recalling brighter hours,
When loved by the monarch—by the monarch of the flowers.
So I a poor robin, caged here so lonely,
Trolling each morning o'er my lay, so homely,
With note long drawn, and thrilling trilling, louder thrilling.
All birds round—list the sound,
But then again—
I dance the saltarella,
And the light tarantella,
Sound the rattling castanet,
Wise in fortunes divination,
I can tell on hand, or cards, what wife, and children you'll get :

I tell your fortune by your face,
Or on your hand your fate I'll trace;
Especially, I can see
                A guinea, for me,
Makes a glorious destiny—
I dispense futurity—
Ac cor-ding-ly.
Pray walk in—now walk in,
The sound of my tamborine—
                Walk in.
All shall know, what they shall know,
Yes,—now walk in,
Ne'er such wonders e'er were seen—
                Walk in.

I, when in gin, have been—
My good friends—my delight
Will be, every night,
To see you, my delight.
Yes, I'm sure you will return
Your fate to learn,
All your hopes to obey,
Is the way—
                I divine.
Can you then, and now deny, what a happy task is mine,
And by my address,
You all must confess,
I have divined—
Your hopes—your mind.
So walk in, &c., &c.

Bel. 'Tis enough—I forgive you—I will no more complain but your old sorcerer, is he your lover still?

Arg. More than before—

Bel. Indeed, I come then just in time.

Arg. But as you have advised, to lull his fears again—feign to lend an ear, as yielding to his will.

Bel. After his love song to you, almost his daughter. I town, what does he?

Arg. Sells the wondrous water-cure.

Bel. Some abomination—filthy and black no doubt; hav you of his receipt, the secret 'ere found out?

Arg. Without a doubt—I know them all.   [MUSIC

DUET.

Listen, here's a water that will cure ye.
    Of everything; to this wond'rous draught all is the same;
'Gainst all ills this water will insure ye.
    It has attained for all a wond'rous fame—

Yes, I assure ye:
    For from the well they drew it, I assure ye, sparkling and
        pure it came.

Bel.	What, water pure?
Arg.	Yes, to be sure.
Bel.	Oh, the vile cheat!
	Always I thought
	I'd catch him out.
Arg.	What's to be done now?
Bel.	Leave me alone now;
	This Charlatan
	Soon will discover
	Unchanged is your lover.
	I have a plan—
	Who's this?
Arg.	'Tis he!

                       [*Exit* BELLONI, U. E. L.

Enter TARTAGLIA *on platform,* R.

Tar. Ah, do my eyes deceive me—it was that scamp, Belloni,
who has slipped away.   . [*comes down.*

Arg. Yes, what eyes you have—what an advantage is that
twist, by which you can see round a corner.

Tar. (enraged) That wretched actor—that miserable Punch
—he follows us from town to town. Is it to make love to
you?

Arg. You must really be a wizard, or the old gentleman—
one or t'other, I'm sure.

Tar. What said he?

Arg. You are a sorcerer, and must know.

Tar. Word for word—out with it.

Arg. That he loves—adores me! and in spite of a brutal,
jealous old hyæna, he will make me his wife.

Tar. Hyæna!

Arg. Yes, he meant you, you know. You see how sincere
I am—aint I?

Tar. Sincere! A hem. And you replied—

Arg. Nothing—I only listened. How could I help it—it
was so interesting.

Tar. (aside). Simple soul! (*Aloud*) You must not, my
angel. Would you accept the offer of this Jack Pudding?

Arg. What, when I am beloved of the mighty Tartaglia,
who, from Rome to Naples, from Genoa to Paris, is known at
the great empiric! Can you suppose it?

Tar. Spare me. Yes, I am a famous man—it is a great
fact. But listen, Argentine. When your worthy and respectable father died in the lazaretto, he made me his sole execu or
and heir; he had nothing to leave but his virtues and your-

self. I accepted the trust. I have watched over your budding
juvenility—I have trained your mind and form, and now I
mean to endow you with immortality. I will give you my
name.

Arg. (*aside*). Two words to that bargain.

Tar. Ha! you smile, my *medicine* Venus. I see, I see,
your little heart has found a home in this capacious bosom.
As for that retailer of other's brains—pha! wisdom before
wit. Then gaze on me; exhibit your taste by preferring the
renowned inventor of the miraculous water—this unique
specimen of man. (*Sees* BELLONI's *booth.*) Ah! what do I
see? (*Cross to booth* L.) Body of Bacchus!

Arg. What is it?

Tar. Toe-nail of Saint Januarius! what do I see; a rival
allowed to establish his rostrum under my very nostrum.
Here's gratitude in the civil authorities, after my pulling out,
gratis, four double teeth from the mayor.

Arg. All sound ones!

Tar. True. But they would have soon spoiled 'em; and
when I, by my cosmetics, cured him of all his grey hairs—

Arg. By leaving him as bald as a sixpence.

Tar. No matter. Range all my pill boxes—quick. I'll
meet this rival, face to face. Have you filled all the bottles
with the wond'rous water?

Arg. I've filled from the pump fifty draughts of it.

Tar. Good; from pump it comes—to pumps it will return.

Arg. Would you like to taste it?

Tar. I drink water! Forbid it, Bacchus—it would poison
me; I should die of water on the chest. Go, I hear the
crowd approaching. Prepare yourself—quick!

[ARGENTINE *exits into booth* R. TARTAGLIA *looks
off, and then exits into booth* R.

CHORUS.

List, my friends, to sweet music's spell,
　Pleasure calls,—let us now obey;
With joyous strain sounds the tarentelle,
　Life's short hours beguile away.

POLICHIELLE *enters on platform,* R. *accompanied by a man
with a trombone.*

And lo! behold Polichinelle
　Invites us all with merry sway;
He will, e'er long, our cares dispel,
　List, my friends, &c. &c.

Enter TARTAGLIA *on platform,* R. *preceded by* ADONIS, *and followed by* ARGANTINE, *who blows the trumpet,*

AIR.—TARTAGLIA.

Here ye are—here ye are—here ye are;
Here's the great Tartaglia—
All ills curing,
Life assuring.
Here's the great Tartaglia;
Medicine—surgery—
Cosmetics, if you fancy—
Boluses—purgery—
There is nought he does not know.
He can quick your fortunes show,
With but a touch of necromancy.
No, ne'er upon this earth below,
Can mankind his equal show.
Now, I pray,
Look this way:
Now, I pray—
I assure ye
This will cure ye.

Cho. Drink, and live for ever. So you may be
Your own posterity.
Drink, live for ever—so we may be
Thus our own posterity,
None e'er have been
So wondrous seen.

Enter BELLONI *on platform,* L. *disguised as Scaramouch, and a large nose on. Punch sounds the gong.*

Tar. Why, who is this I see?
Arg. Oh, heaven! 'tis Belloni.
Bel. Listen to me—
In silence, since
Of phlebotony
I'm the Prince.
Here you will find, a radical cure
For all complaints man can endure,
I've notes from earls, and dukes, no less,
See my advertisement in the morning press.

CHORUS.

Then let us hear
In silence, since
Of doctors wise,
He is the prince!

Bel.　　　　　　What you here behold,
　　　　　　　　Oh wondrous to think;
　　　　　　　　Of this water drink,—
　　　　　　　　You'll never grow old.

Tar.　　Oh nothing can beat
　　　　　That young scamps pretension,
　　　　　His wondrous invention,
　　　　　Is nought but a cheat!
　　　　　Stay awhile—yes stay—stay awhile—stay awhile,
　　　　　As I live on the earth, that's under us,
　　　　　The genuine water so wondrous,
　　　　　Here ye are good folks—here ye are!
　　　　　It is that of Tartaglia!

Bel.　Yes, 'tis true, his is the genu-*ine*.

Tar.　Ha—now hear ye!

Bel.　'Tis true—but mine
　　　　　Is the same precisely.

Tar.　Precisely!—what, you have the face—

Bel.　The same receipt as you sir, I know.

Tar.　A falsehood,

Bel.　As I can shew.

Tar.　Impossible! he'll do you nicely—

[TARTAGLIA *and* BELLONI *descend from their platforms, and meet in* c.

　　　　　To prove at once his false pretension,
　　　　　I dare him, and now to mention
　　　　　This receipt—so let him prepare.
　　　　　At once my secret to declare,
　　　　　How do I this wondrous draught compose.

Cho.　How does he this, &c.

Tar.　This offer you think fair, I suppose,
　　　　　Let him but tell the secret rare,
　　　　　Henceforth all my fortune he shall share.

Bel.　What you insist?　　　　　　　　[*he repeats.*

Tar.　Ah, I'm caught.
　　　　　What—water pure—can you believe this vile imposter here?

Cho.　'Tis false! 'tis false! the thing is clear.

Tar.　And so he would have you believe,
　　　　　That all this time I could deceive
　　　　　You all, and rob you of your pence.

Cho.　Yes, yes, he is a cheat,
　　　　　And his purposes we'll defeat.

[*They drive* BELLONI *over the platform,* L. *tear down his sign, and pelt him with stones, bottles, &c.* BELLONI *puts up his umbrella to protect himself, and runs off,* U. E. R. *followed by the Chorus.*

Tar. Ha! ha! ha! So the rascal's beaten, and no easy matter—the joke was getting rather too good.

Arg. Poor Belloni!

Tar. Belloni! 'twas he then?

Arg. Yes, Belloni. The famous Scaramouch.

Tar. Famous! Ah, but I had him just now—a pretty fool, as if he could persuade people, that they were as big asses as himself—not but what they are. But no matter, we are rid of him, for after such a deception, I dont think he'll dare oppose his nose to mine—remain here—I'm going into work, if you miss my company, call me. [*Exit into booth,* R.

Arg. Thank you, but the farther you are off the more agreeable the prospect. Not so with my charming young lover—his touching eloquence finds easy access to my heart, which gladly opens for the reception of his love. If I am forced to marry this odious bubble of a doctor, let him beware, for my vengeance shall be terrible.

SONG.

When wed with one, the affection binding.
In ev'ry glance we mutual joy betray,
In our hearts, each wish an echo finding.
The others will, we cheerfully obey.
When tied to one we do detest,
The face in smiles is never drest,
Or to the view he seems a pest.
How we pine day by day,
And to die how we pray.
Each moment we grow more perverse,
The temper growing worse and worse.
How we vex,
Him perplex,
Be a perfect shrew.
And to enrage him, is our great delight,
To worry him from morn to night,
Yes, all he shall rue.

When near to those, we are with fondness living,
The wealth of worlds is nought compared to this,
To please but him, and thus devotion proving,
The true heart's deaf to others vows of bliss.
But with a husband we despise,
Then other forms attract our eyes,
To him list with a smile,
Our hearts would beguile.
Caring not for our good name,
If for conquests we have the fame.
Spouse with eyes,
Jealous spies,
Disgrace in view.

But to enrage him is our sole delight.
To worry him from morn to night;
  Yes all he shall rue.

Enter BELLONI, U. E. R.

Bel. Hist! Argentine.

Arg. Ah! it is he.

Bel. Your own, Belloni. Is that old rhinoceros there?

Arg. Hush! yes.

Bel. Then all's right.

Arg. What would you do?

Bel. (tenderly.) Anything to show my adoration of you. Tell me I'm an ugly villain—that you hate me, and won't marry me—every thing but the truth.

Arg. Why—what for?

Bel. Be firm; my angel, spread your wings and fly me; call out—box my ears, that he may hear you. Let your indignation bawl out at the top of your voice.

Arg. Shall I begin by boxing your ears?

Bel. Try the other effect first.

Arg. I obey.

A TRIO.

BELLONI, ARGENTINE, TARTAGLIA, *who peeps on from booth,* R.

Arg.	Leave me, sir, I pray,
Bel.	Hear me, fair one.
Arg.	No, no, you must begone.
Tar.	Yes, 'tis he—
	This actor's daring,
	Is beyond bearing.
Arg.	He over hears me;
Bel.	Yes, I see thus that he fears me.
Arg.	Now begone.
Bel.	Dearest appease thee—
Arg.	'Tis vain you ask a kiss—now begone.
Bel.	Ah, do but bless me with a kiss:
Tar.	It is to please me.
	From fear now this frees me,
	What happiness,
	A kiss, no more, but a kiss.
Arg.	What more to me have you to say,
	Can I not your suit rebuff—
	At my feet your heart you lay,
	I pray, sir, is there more of this precious stuff?
Bel.	No, 'tis not all,
Arg.	'Tis quite enough.
Bel.	Is then your heart to love closed ever,
	Ah! no, no, no, I feel its spell.
	But to thee may I hope never,

Arg.   I love and whom, you know too well.
         Of him I love one hope I prove
         That ere long you will see
            The contract signing,
            Two fond hearts twining,
         A happy wife will be.

Bel.   And he you love, one hope will prove,
         That ere long you will see
            The contract signing.
            Two fond hearts twining,
         The happy wife you will be.

Tar.   And he you love, &c. &c.

TARTAGLIA *advances.*

Arg.   And are you satisfied with that, sir?

Tar.   You see she has refused you flat, sir,

Bel.   And is it you who rob me of my bliss?

Tar.   Where could she choose better, sir, then this?

Arg.   Ah, why then this should you surprise,
            Look at his face,
            Behold his grace,
            Nought can efface,
            And a scarecrow,
            He is my joy,
            My blooming boy,
            Love sans alloy,
            I now shall know.
   And so you made sure I would not refuse you,
   And so you made sure my folly would choose you,
   Because you think you're handsome young and bold,
   And he is vilely ugly, fat, and old,
   Still to my breast that form I soon will fold.
   Oh what a nose! oh what a face,
   Who could suppose he had such grace.

Tar. Look at my nose, look at my face,
   Who could suppose I had such grace.

Bel. Look at his nose, look at his face,
            &c. &c.

Arg. I shall soon be united—who could prevent my only trust,
   All his address, and his face, bring to bear he must.

Tar. Soon my fond love will be returned.
   Forbid the bands, I'll give you freely leave
   To try if you Tartaglia can deceive.

Bel. Yes, too well I know all hope within me dying,
     Oh, my despair you will soon see deadly prove.
   When in the grave you see Belloni lying,
     Weep o'er the bier of one, who died of love.

All. Look at his nose, look at his face,
            &c. &c.

[*Exit* BELLONI, U. E. L., *kissing his hand to* ARGENTINE.

Arg. What amusing despair ! his eyes rolled as if he had been galvanized.

Tar. My dear, love is a kind of electric fluid.

Arg. Oh ! what a battery you must be. '

Tar. Intelligent soul !

Arg. What droll fish disappointed lovers are.

Tar. Yes, a sort of flounder—he seemed stark-staring mad.

Arg. Ah, he did, indeed. (*significantly.*)

Tar. But his disappointment may render him dangerous.

Arg. Insure your life Guardy for my sake.

Tar. You can't against a stiletto, dearest—his violence may drive him to commit some desperate act.

[*Both laughing immoderately.*

Arg. It may—it will—oh ! my foreboding heart—assassination was in his glance—he looked daggers.

Tar. Don't, love, you derange my nervous system.

Arg. (*aside*) If I can but frighten him into giving his consent—

Tar. To prevent his destroying our relative positions we must be made one directly.

Arg. (*aside*) Heavens ! that's not what I want.

Tar. Go and adorn your precious person, and dress your face in its sweetest smiles, and I'll hasten to the Podesta for the contract, that is to unite in one flame our two burning hearts.

Arg. (*aside*) Oh, I'm a lost young woman.

Tar. Don't let your happiness overpower you—I shall soon return—adieu !

Arg. Never, I hope—adieu !   [*Exit* R.

Tar. Ha, ha! poor little thing! how she loves me—it is miraculous the respect talent has upon woman. I have only to fix my eye on a girl so—she's facinated—mesmerized ! Young lovers may swear, threaten, pray, kneel, she hears nothing! she yields—then she is an immolation on the altar of science, a new triumph of art over nature !

Enter BELLONI, U. E. L., *very pale.*

Bel. Tartaglia !

Tar. Belloni !

Bel. His last appearance in that character—

Tar. How pale he is !

Bel. Hoh! heh! heh ! (*grimaces*)

Tar. What is it ?

Bel. You a doctor, and cannot tell—hoh! observe—heh ! you have—have—hoh! killed me.

Tar. I kill anybody—impossible! I'm a singular instance to the contrary in the medical profession—I constitute the exception which proves the rule !

Bel. Listen !

Tar. I do.

Bel. Look!

Tar. I see—

Bel. A dead man!—a fact—as sure as I'm alive—I have just swallowed one pound of ratsbane.

Tar. A pound!

Bel. Avoudupois!

Tar. And you still live?

Bel. A little—not worth mentioning—hih—hoh—oh! I'm, I'm going!

Tar. How he gnashes! what a fearful case—what can I do for you?

Bel. I came here to—to—oh! to make my will—all I have I—oh—oh—to Argentine!

Tar. All you have you owe—but all you have at present, is a pain in your Biliary ducts.

Bel. And thirty thousand crowns.

Tar. Thirty thousand crowns—and you have made your will.

Bel. No.

Tar. Not made it—but there may not be time to get it drawn out.

Bel. What's to be done—how can Argentine inherit all my wealth.

Tar. Have you no sister.

Bel. No!

Tar. No brother.

Bel. No!

Tar. No father.

Bel. No!

Tar. No mother.

Bel. No!

Tar. How then did you come into the world.

Bel. I was won at a raffle—oh—oh!

Tar. Stay—I have it. The Podesta will be here in a few minutes, with a marriage contract.

Bel. (*aside,*) Ha! ha! he bites.

Tar. If instead of me, you marry Argentine—

Bel. Marry her!

Tar. You'll do me the favor to die at your earliest convenience after the ceremony—

Bel. I'll be punctual—oh!

Tar. (*calls*) Adonis the arm-chair, Argentine.

ADONIS *enters,* R., *places arm-chair,* C. *Exits* R.

TRIO.

Tar. Argentine—here; Argentine—quick, away.

ARGENTINE *enters*, R.

Arg.   What is your will?
Tar.   You shall know it;
         But, oh, my dearest, cherished ward,
         If you love me, pray now show it.
         Deign to accord me now the strongest proof of your
            regard.
Arg.   A proof of my regard—how to do that?
Tar.   Despair has smote—
         A victim here behold.
Arg.   I see.
Tar.   By love and rat's-bane sold.
Arg.   Oh, heavens!   Am I an antidote?
Tar.   Sole heiress of his wealth, 'tis true,
         After his death he would make you.
Arg.   When he is dead I wish no more.
Tar.   Can you refuse him at death's door—
         Oh! here behold at death's door lying,
         Your poor young lover now is dying;
         Would you your real affection prove,
         Grant this last favor to you love.
Bel.   Oh here behold at death's door lying,
         Your poor young lover now is dying,
         Would you your true affection prove,
         Grant this last favor to your love.
Arg.   Oh here behold at death's door lying,
         My poor lover now is dying,
         I would my true affection prove,
         And show my duty to my own love.
Tar.   This is not all.
Arg.   What, is there more?
Tar.   'Tis but a trifle.
         You must straight wed him.
Arg.   Wed him?   Oh, father.
Tar.   Yes; I know too well how you him abhor.
         Oh, for my sake you will not refuse;
         So pray consent—you can't but choose.
         Oh, here behold, &c.

Enter PODESTA, *with portfolio, pen, ink, and a contract.* U.E.L.

Pod.   My function here to exercise,
            I come.
Tar.   Your worship we have sought.
Pod.   What for?
Tar.   The contract have you brought?
Pod.   Eh!
Tar.   The banns, we need not advertise.

Pod.   What do you say?

Arg.
Bel.& } He nothing hears of what ^{we} say.
Tar.

(correcting) He nothing hears of what we/you say.

Arg.
and } The contract—quick!
Tar.

Pod.   Oh, that's it! I have got it here—We'll all arrange.
       The names will change.

Tar.   With haste I pray that you will.

Pod.   What's that? I have forgot the names—what, I, who
       dares to say?

Arg.
Bel.& } He nothing hears of what we say—
Tar. The contract quick—the names you'll change.

Pod.   Ah! good, very well, the names we'll change.
       Now say, which is the bride?

Tar.   Its just the same—She's at your side.

Arg.   Argentine Diavolini.

Pod.   'Tis well, the names are here, I see,
       And the bride-groom, where is he?

Bel.   *(grimaces)* I am he.

Pod.   Oh, horror! for heavens sake, how dread!
       Be quick! he's almost dead.

Bel.   Ja-co-po Belloni.

Pod.   Sign this, madame—you sign there, and now Mister
       guardian.

Tar.   There, its done.

All.   There, its done.   [to die.

Bel.   Oh dear, I sink with pain, its now all over, I am going

Tar.   How very kind he did postpone his death awhile till all
          was done,
       Oh, poor Belloni.

Bel.   Oh, how I burn, a little water I pray;

Arg.   Drink here, drink deep, and may it cure;
       Yes, drink, it is the wond'rous water—

Bel.   I drink.

Tar.   Yes,

Bel.   The wond'rous water pure.

Tar.   Yes, that will give you ease I think.

Bel.   Oh, prodigious! what means this cure
      All at once. I cease to sink,
    Tell me I am not dreaming sure
      While upon the grave's dark brink,
    Thus that I am saved most wondrously.

Tar.   You're cure, 'tis false, a brazen lie,
      He swore most solemnly to die.

Bel.   How am I cured?

Cho.	'Tis the water cure
	Which you said was pure
	Of great Tartaglia.
Tar.	With fury I shall choke—
Bel.	With fury he will choke.
Tar.	This is beyond a joke,
Bel.	Indeed it was a joke,
Cho.	Honor and praise to the doctor.
Bel.	Let us be friendly, and henceforth let fair play—
Arg.	Dear guardian, hear me, but a word to say—
Bel.	Between us let from hence peace ever be,
Arg.	I only ask this once to wed Belloni.
Bel.	For if my trick robs you of such a wife,
	Think that a cure will last you all your life.
Arg.	You've honor, riches, still on your side,
	Then consent, and bless now the bride.
Tar.	Riches, honor, well in the end will I win,
	And so to lose no time my harvest I'll begin.

[TARTAGLIA *stands in the chair to sell his wonderful water.*

CHORUS.

Drink, live for ever! so all may be
Thus their own posterity.
Nought has been
So wondrous seen.
To the great doctor hail!
All hail! all hail!

R.   *Disposition of Characters.*   L.

PEOPLE. LEONI, ARGENTINE, TARTAGLIA, PODESTA. PEOPLE.

W. S. JOHNSON, "Nassau Steam Press," 60, St. Martin's Lane.